Over 40? Get that

CW00431027

To my family and friends, thank you for your support.

To Adam and Josh, you mean everything to me.

CONTENTS

INTRODUCTION

Over 40 and dating again!

Sally and Darren had sex. Nothing remarkable in that, they'd known each other for years, although they'd only exchanged a handful of words during all that time. Darren was a local business man Sally occasionally bumped into, they'd chat and flirt a bit, but that was it. Then one day, Darren asked Sally out for a drink, one thing led to another and need I say more. It was wild passion, the build-up of all the flirting over the years only adding to the magnetism between them. Over the next couple of weeks, they met several times, had dinner, then fell into bed.

After two weeks, Darren's calls ceased. Sally texted him, received a brief reply and then nothing. Darren had, by all accounts, removed himself from the situation. Sally, on the other hand had not. Her mind worked overtime, what had she said or done wrong? She replayed the scenes in her mind, analysing every moment, checked her phone every two minutes and felt rising anxiety, she'd gone from Woman Desired to Woman Deleted. All too familiar in your 20s or 30s, but Sally was 52, she should have known better. Problem was she'd forgotten. For the last 25 years she'd been married, now she was divorced and plunged headlong into a dating world which was completely alien.

We've all been there. I know I have. We know, every time a woman sleeps with a man, and it doesn't matter who he is - good, bad or ugly, she bonds with him. The more sex you have with him, the more the bond strengthens, and it doesn't matter how old you are, the mistakes are still there to be made. So, this is a book to guide you patently but with some **Tough Love**, through the world of dating for the over 40s. A dating world that is not as it was in the 1980s. At this point you may be asking yourself, why should I listen to Jacqui van Loen? Who the heck is she? Well I'm over 50, divorced, two fabulous kids, a Master's Degree in Psychology and have spent a lot of my teaching career - between teaching GCSE and 'A' Level - setting up single colleagues before going on to set up my own successful matchmaking business.

My life wasn't planned this way. I was planning to marry a millionaire with his own yacht, we'd summer in Nice, winter in Barbados. Unfortunately, someone forgot to tell the millionaire about his princess living and waiting in Essex! So, I married Joe Schmoe, had kids, got divorced and set out to find someone I could love, who would treat me well and with whom I could have a good life. I feel I've met every type of man, tall good-looking ones who couldn't string a sentence together, short muscular ones who spoke in loud voices and drank too much, those who clearly didn't have any dress sense and those who after two minutes, made me want to walk away – briskly! Oh yes indeed, the dating journey, when you're over 40 is not smooth. And it's not as if there are no self-help books out there - look no further than Amazon and click on any one of over 121,000 books on dating. They range through 'Dating for Dummies' to 'Break up to Make up" and 'How to Get Your Ex Back', all books you could and may have read in your twenties. But being twenty and dating is not the same as being over forty and dating. Why? Because who we are now isn't who we were then. We've been around the block, we may have kids, a house, assets, a job, family ties, not to mention the dog or any other animals acquired along the way. In other words, we've been there, we've done it, we have the scars and we're wearing the t-shirt.

Dating has changed, in fact, while you were looking the other way, everything changed. Nowadays it's not so much an introduction by friends, meeting someone in a bar at a party, or simply bumping into someone nice who asks you to go for a coffee. No, dating has become a lesson in technology. Indeed, a twentysomething once asked me "How do you meet anyone if you're not online?" To which I added "Especially when you've spent the last 20 years married and bringing up a family." The daunting fact is more people are single now than ever before, we're all (thanks to technology) more accessible to reach, yet, oddly enough, at 40 or above it seems the pool of dating possibilities is ever decreasing.   This book is the accumulation of experience allied with psychological insight. It also offers a path to building confidence and self-esteem. It aims to give you the route map to find someone you enjoy spending time with and with whom you can build a future, at the same time as maintaining happiness and security within yourself.

I have found asking people what they do to attract someone, results only in a comment that's clearly unreliable or vague. The best way to answer that question is through observation and I have watched and learned from the best. As a psychologist, I am always interested in people's behaviour but never so much as by those who are trying to attract a mate, it's fascinating.

You may not agree with everything I say, I'm used to that, many people want my advice but not everyone wants to act on it. You will find this book illustrates that there are many ways to catch a fish but ensuring it's the fish you truly want to have dinner with, is harder. There's more written about love than any other subject and I promise to try not to bore or patronise, because once you've reached your 40s or beyond, you'll have seen and heard more crap that you ever thought possible. What I will tell you is what I've learned by reading, watching and talking to women who have been in your shoes and met the partner they always wanted to meet.   Within this book we're going to look at issues such as:

- Will I ever find anyone again?
- Why we fall in love with some people and not others.
- Obstacles to finding love in the first place.
- Why do I always go for the type who isn't any good for me?
- Where do I meet people to grow a social life?
- My children don't want me to date, but I've got to get out of the house.
- My children do want me to meet someone.
- I haven't got the body I once had.
- I'm scared to have sex with someone new.
- I've no idea how to talk to someone else.
- I've lost my self-confidence.
- I don't feel I'm the least bit interesting.
- I want to go out but haven't got anyone to go with.
- I don't want to come over as desperate.
- How do I flirt, I feel I've lost the skill?
- I've been focused on my career, I feel I've missed the boat.
- I need to meet someone of the same faith.

- I'm not attracted to men of my own age, I want to date someone younger to reflect how I feel.
- Dating is such a meat market.
- I feel emotionally damaged from my last relationship.
- I want to find my mojo.

So, if you're still with me, let's go!

Ethel's finding new romance a little overwhelming.

©Create Communication 2019

SECTION 1

Romantic love and its problems

One of the most important principles for choosing a partner sensibly is not to be in a hurry. Being single and comfortable in your own skin is a vital precondition of being satisfied within a relationship. No-one can choose wisely when remaining single feels unbearable. We need to be at peace with the fact we may have to spend years of solitude in order to have any chance of forming a good relationship.

Unfortunately, after a certain age, namely your 20s, society makes being single feel unpleasant. If it's unpleasant at 30 it can sometimes seem unbearable after 40. People in couples are often too threatened by the independence of the single person to invite them round very often - and definitely not on a Saturday night. When I was first single after my divorce, I found I was only invited at lunchtime and then hurried out the door if my friend's husband arrived. As if I would really want to jump him! It is no wonder when someone even slightly decent comes along we cling on to them, sometimes at eventual enormous cost.

Being single isn't the horrible condition society would have us or others believe. In fact, only when we're secure, happy and fulfilled as a single, will we know we're choosing someone to pair up with for the right reasons. At that point, we'll be ready to be with someone based on their own merits, not just because they're free and we might then be welcomed back to the Saturday night dinner scene.

Of course, one of the main problems is finding someone special. We know we don't fall in love with just anyone: we're led by our types. We're drawn to people who fit our ideal. This assumption of course is badly flawed, because being led by our instinct means we reject perfectly good guys who on paper sound great but don't float our boat when we meet them. As a matchmaker, this is the number one obstacle for getting people out on dates. They read the profile that says that the other person has all the qualities the client asked for and on meeting, the client turns her nose up. She may say "It doesn't feel right." or "I don't like their nose or He's not tall/slim/good looking enough". We are very choosy.

Choosiness has become a problem because of romanticism, which we have been fed in spades. From Jane Austin to Walt Disney, we girls have been dealt a daily dose of finding the one. 'Mr Darcy, if you're out there, wring out that shirt, find me now and take me away from this life!'

Choosiness has led us to reject people without any particular flaw, we may say too nice or bit boring without thinking further. Why do we do that when they may possibly be perfect for us? The reason is rooted in the need for familiarity. Adult love is wrapped up in the love we had as a child, therefore picking a partner has to re-evoke the love felt when we were young and living with our parents. Rejecting someone is code for 'They don't remind me of feeling loved." We want a partner who feels familiar, even if this means being with someone who causes us pain. For example, we may be drawn to someone who bosses us around or doesn't pay us too much attention. This is because past patterns, laid down in childhood, inform us this is familiar and because of that familiarity we feel a close bond with this person.

We repeatedly go for relationships with partners who are flawed in nature, who don't allow us to flourish and all because this type of love feels familiar and therefore must be right. The author and joint founder of The School of Life, Alain de Botton calls this The Repetition Dynamic, it is the tendency to repeatedly go for partners who we chose at an unconscious level because of the relationships we had with our parents as a child. If the affection we knew as a child is connected to some kind of pain, we tend to recognize that pain as love. We yearn for a partner to feel familiar, even if this means we choose someone connected with past unhappy circumstances.

On the other hand, we may go for someone who is completely different from our parents. In fact, we may recoil from those who remind us of them in any way. We try to escape from bad points that are so apparent to us, but this can be a major problem because by recoiling from the bad, we also dismiss the good. We may have had a parent who was creative but had a terrible temper. Now, we dismiss anyone we consider creative, or maybe you meet someone who is good with money, but you dismiss them because you fear they also have the trait of being humiliating.

Either way, repeating or recoiling we're on loser street. We need to forget about romanticism and be a little more down to earth when it comes to picking a partner. We need to understand we ourselves are flawed, and so therefore is everyone else. Once we understand we all have faults, but at the same time can love ourselves, we're able to look at people in different ways, see the faults and still love them. My Own Weaknesses?

Example: I make quick decisions without thinking things through.

1.

2.

3.

4.

5.

I Can't Find Anyone!

Really! We live on a planet of 7.53 billion people there must be someone. In fact, there are plenty of people, it's just that often we're unable to see opportunities that may be staring us in the face. Apart from being choosy we also believe there is no one out there quite good enough. We feel we could do better and of course we never do. Here is a little bit of **Tough Love, we really need to take an honest look at ourselves.** Are we really as precious, deserving and special as we think we are? No of course not. We are a bit nuts, sometimes too proud, we can be argumentative, laughable and at times, bloody ridiculous. Of course, we've never been told these faults because our parents were too kind and our friends didn't want to upset us.

We might be a proper pain in the backside; we don't like doing things differently; we don't like having to back down; we don't listen very well; we struggle to share responsibility; we're demanding and sometimes not good at communicating. Only by realising we're far from perfect can we be liberated to get together with others who are imperfect too. Taking a leap in the dark, acknowledging our own faults means we revise our view of ourselves and that can in itself nurture confidence.

When we're realistic about ourselves we have a far more realistic view of others. This leads on to taking a better look at someone who previously might have been not quite right. If we look beneath the surface, we can far better understand what else is going on with that person. Just because someone looks conventional doesn't mean that he doesn't have a wild side or a that a guy who maybe isn't the best looking in the world may be one of the kindest people you'll ever meet. His job may not be impressive, but maybe he loves the outdoors - just like you. Looking beyond the obvious at things we don't immediately take to, allows us to be more open minded. Ultimately the essence of love is adoration mixed with toleration.

Romanticism tends to declare the only sound foundation for a relationship is an intense bond of love. The idea being when we meet *The One* we instantly know it. We're all aware of the being-in-love symptoms - can't sleep, butterflies in the tummy, checking the phone every 5 minutes, However, intellectually we know very well, love doesn't usually hit like a lightning bolt. We need to be realistic in assessing ourselves and others and bring that realism to our understanding of a relationship.

Now whilst I've said we're not necessarily going to look for potential partners based on looks, I'm going to make a completely contradictory point. We have to look the best we can out there in the dating world. Why? Mainly because people (not as enlightened) make up their minds about someone within the first 6 seconds of meeting. They look with their eyes and not their imagination. They look at the packaging, not what's inside.   Guys find a woman's face the most important consideration, even more so than her body. They also like high heels, stockings and suspenders - just what you need at 40 while doing the ironing! Some things just never change! However, whilst I hesitate to comment on stockings and suspenders, I can share some general thoughts. Take a look at Jodie Foster or Julianne Moore, both over 50 and not although classically beautiful, they are attractive. I always think you should look good for the decade you're in. So, when you're embarking on the dating scene: you need to look great and feel confident because you want to attract the same.

Take a good look in the mirror

There are times when I look in the mirror and see someone who quite frankly could have just emerged (and not unscathed!) from the Crimea War. It seems that once you get past 40 everything you thought you could rely on body-wise, puts two fingers up at you. You look in the mirror to see, well, certainly not the girl you once were. I personally can see my boobs looking at my feet, lips going thin and hips expanding. Worse still, my jawline is on its way down too. This unfortunately is the decade of reality.

And things don't stand still. From 50, collagen breaks down, so skin loses thickness and support structure. Neck skin gets thinner and your hair becomes finer. In your 60s, skin cells have 30 per cent less natural moisture and will feel drier, thinner, tighter and flakier. What can you do? Well certainly don't despair and for goodness sake don't rush to the nearest plastic surgeon in the hopes of becoming a whole new you. As I say, you should aim to look good for the decade you're in. Cosmetic surgery and recovery is an extremely emotional undertaking. If you're thinking of going under the knife, think very carefully. Why are you doing it? Having your breasts enlarged or your face hauled back, isn't going to stop time or bring the love of your life to the doorstep. Far more hope of that comes when you start to take better care of yourself. You'll immediately reap the benefits; your confidence will shine through and this is by far the most attractive thing you can give yourself and others.

Let's make a start on you. Take a deep breath and rate how you feel about yourself:

Rate your features out of 10 (1 low, 10 high)

	Rate how you feel about it out of 10 (1 low, 10 high)
Hair condition	
Hair style	
Hair colour	
Eyebrows	
Eyelids	
Lips	
Teeth	
Nails	
Weight	
Feet	
Posture	
Breast size	
Breast shape	
Bum	
Tummy	
Arms	

You now have a list of things you like, others you're not so keen on but can live with and those you want to change. Next steps?

Well the good news is we live in a world where everything can be fixed. You can approach it in various ways: a good old-fashioned skin-care routine, exercise and plenty of fruit and veg, or for bits that need more help, the plastic surgeon, although as I've said previously, looking good comes from inside and surgeons aren't miracle workers. Start to take care of yourself, the better you feel the more you'll pull other people towards you because confidence is attractive.

Doris has taken up weight lifting as part of her 5-point Plan to Physical Fitness.

©Create Communication.2019

A Five-Point Plan to Physical Confidence

Decide: What you want, what you need and how you can do it. It's all about prioritising. You can't do it all at once, so start with the lowest ratings on your list or on the ones that you feel most adversely affect you.

Where: Look at where you can go to rectify the problem. For example, if losing hair is causing you anxiety then your first stop might be a specialist hair clinic in London. On the other hand, if you've had the same hairstyle for years and want a change, head for a different hairdresser, a fresh point of view can work wonders for your look.

Who: Ask for personal recommendations. If you're looking for a great eyebrow shape, ask friends whose eyebrows you envy, who they'd recommend or head for local social media and ask for recommendations, you'll be surprised at how many people will respond.

When: If it's important, take the time to do it. If you want to have a colour, cut, wash and blow dry you'll need a good couple of hours to relax and enjoy it. On the other hand, if you're going the full hog and have a facelift, you need to book a couple of weeks off work.

How: Where there's a will there's a way. You might need to save up to make yourself over, but there are always things you can do that don't take too much cash. For instance, you can magic up some homemade hair conditioner with some olive oil and an avocado.

Note, the part I've deliberately left out is the Why. Why you want to do anything to your body is entirely up to you, but losing a partner and wanting to find a new one is definitely a good enough incentive to want to look the very best you can.

Simple Steps

Here's a few tips which I hope don't sound patronising and if it does then I apologise in advance now!

Hair: Well-groomed hair instantly makes you feel gorgeous. It's a bit of a myth that we need to cut our hair short as we get older, so unless you have a petite pixie face, forget it. It can really age you and show up a not-so-taut jawline. In fact, if you've put some weight on, short hair can age you dreadfully.

Men like long hair, according to the Daily Mail (2008), the Pixie Crop only got 7 per cent of the vote and the *bob* didn't score highly either, which is surprising because personally I think short hair can look fabulous on some face shapes. A report by Hinsz, Matz and Patience showed hair length and quality can act as a cue to men on a woman's youth and health. *(Journal of Experimental Social Psychology Volume 37, issue 2, March 2001 P 1666-172).* In other words, men judge a woman's age and health on the quality of her hair.

To create a mane that's heading towards fullness and shine, deep-condition. You can do this at home. We all know you need to shampoo and then condition, but I'm not talking about the 20 seconds you have the conditioner on in the shower, but regular deep conditioning treatments to restore shine and give you a smooth texture. You can either deep condition once a week or every time you wash your hair. Frequency of use will depend on your routine and your hair's needs. If you blow dry, use straighteners or other heat treatments you may find you need to apply a treatment 2 – 3 times a week, if you use styling tools and products sparingly, you may only need a treatment once a month. Make it part of your routine and you'll see the benefits within a short space of time.

Colour: As we get older our hair loses colour, some women prefer to leave their hair grey which is fine if it suits you, otherwise it can make you look older. However, be cautious with colour, go lighter than you would have done in your 30s, a dark block colour can make you look like Morticia from the Addams Family whereas some blondes turn you into Barbie's mother. Go to the hairdresser and browse through the colour book. Highlights are great even if you are dark. Have them on the crown area and let it cover the top of your head, giving light colour around the face. Caramel highlights, even if you're brunette can make all the difference, giving the impression of volume and a lift to your face making you look younger. Have a chat with the hairdresser, get some ideas, then take the plunge.

Skin Care: There's no point putting a load of paint onto a canvas with problems. It won't look good, it will look caked. Same with skin which needs more attention once you hit 40 and beyond. The benefits of regular cleansing, toning and moisturising are a given, but you don't need to spend a fortune on products. Firstly, I would highly recommend exfoliation. It helps all products work better and unless you've been advised otherwise, you should exfoliate every day. Don't be harsh by rubbing and rubbing, you're not cleaning pots and pans, just removing dead skin cells, so take care. You can use a washcloth and a little bit of white sugar/salt or an over-the-counter facial exfoliator (make sure it doesn't have plastic microbeads).

From the age of 40 I started to wear a serum or an oil beneath my moisturiser, day and night. Your night-time moisturiser should be heavier than your day-time one, because it has more time to sink into the skin. If you have dehydrated skin, any moisturiser will plump it up and instantly make it look and feel less dry and lined, whether it has cost you £3 or £100.

Sunscreen: The most important thing to put on your face, wear it daily even in Winter. Instead of having a separate sunscreen and moisturizer choose a moisturizer that has an SPF in it. They should also have UVA/UVB protection. What do all these abbreviations mean? SPF (Sun protection factor) is a measure of how long the sunscreen will protect you from ultraviolet B (UVB) rays that will damage your skin and cause it to burn. Ideally choose a moisturiser with SPF30. UVA are rays that penetrate deeper into your skin and are responsible for premature ageing, such as dark spots and wrinkles. The sun is damaging and our skin, no matter how much care we take, will age, why would you want to help that process along? Wearing sunscreen slows down the development of wrinkled, premature aging skin. It also decreases your chance of getting skin cancer, facial brown spots, red veins, blotchiness and skin discolorations. All good reasons to slap it on. Many people say they need the sun to obtain vitamin D, but you can get this by other means such as a healthy vitamin D rich diet of fish, milk, dairy, liver and eggs. If you don't want to wear the white sunscreen, try a tinted one.

Botox® and fillers: Love 'em or hate 'em they have become the mainstay to reverse and theoretically rejuvenate tired-looking faces. Basically, if it moves you can have it immobilised, if it deflates, it can be re-filled, and if it droops, it can be lifted.

The global market for cosmetic fillers to plump up wrinkles and lines, create cheekbones and reshape chins will be worth approximately £7.2 billion by 2023. *(https://www.newswire.com/news/ global-facial-injectables-market-is-expected-to-worth-7-2-billion-by-19587787)* Although there isn't room to go into this in great depth, if you're considering going down this route, do thoroughly research the doctor you're choose. Their qualifications and experience are as important as is setting your own expectations realistically. Go for a consultation which is usually free and if you're not inspired with confidence and have all your questions answered to your satisfaction, you're not obliged to go through with it and would be far better advised to look elsewhere.

Wendy Lewis, author of Plastic makes perfect tells us that Botox® is not a filler, it relaxes muscles to make lines disappear and can slow down the formation of new lines.

Fillers on the other hand temporarily plump up creases but don't prevent them from getting deeper or stop new ones from forming. With fillers, your muscles are still fully active. Fillers add volume to the face, Botox® doesn't. I think Botox® and fillers are great, however keep your expectations realistic; having treatments can make you feel confident and boost your self-esteem, they are not going to transform your life, only you can do that.

Eyes: The eye make-up you used when you were in your 20s and 30s will probably not work for you now. The sparkly shadow that highlighted your eyes 10 years ago will now fall comfortably into the wrinkles and highlight them instead. The dark eyeliner that used to make your eyes look mysterious will now make you look like someone going to a 1960s fancy dress party.

First look at your eyebrows, buy yourself a good eyebrow pencil which matches your tones and fill in the areas that are now thinner and patchy. You might even consider having semi-permanent make-up, which will give your brows a whole new look and lift your face. I would recommend this, because I did this myself, brows will help to shape your face and give definition. There are plenty of people who do semi-permanent make-up, read the reviews and go for a consultation first.

Body: When I ask women what they're most worried about, many say they don't have the body they once did, they're worried about how they look and what impression they make. As you know, I'm going to be straight with you, as we get older there is, naturally, wear and tear on the body so it would be very odd if you still had the body you did at 20. Having children and comfort eating (two things which often go together!) also don't help. However, it is a fact that your shape from the waist down has a lot to do with genetics and hormones. Every woman is born with a certain body type and develops different levels of body fat and muscle mass in accordance. If you were lucky enough to win the gene pool lottery, jolly good for you, but lots of us didn't. There is a certain truth that those of us who look slimmer also look younger, not always but it certainly gives a more youthful look, plus being a few pounds slimmer gives you confidence and that's really what it's all about. Many women I meet have beautiful faces but honestly, could lose a few pounds if not a stone or two. There I've said it, the **Tough Love** bit, lose weight and you will feel a whole lot better - clothes will not only fit but you'll have more clothing options, you'll have more energy, you'll feel back in control and become more confident especially when it comes to having sex with that really hot guy you are going to meet!

So, what can you do? Well there's the gym, sensible eating plan, personal trainers, or you can go the surgical way and have liposuction, tummy tuck, lower body lift, thigh lift, buttock lift, gastric band and even a vaginal rejuvenation. Blimey! Whatever works for you is fine, if you're happy as you are – great, if not I would always recommend the natural way of eating less and exercising more but that's just me, do what makes you happy with yourself. By the way, before you go gung-ho into any kind of exercise see a doctor if you're worried. There's no point in signing up for an intense exercise class if you have a weak heart!

So, don't overdo it, take it slow and steady when you first start out.

According to the Organisation for Economic Co-operation and Development (OECD) 63% of adults considered to be overweight. Those are not great figures, especially now with a report saying that 1 in 20 cancers in the UK are linked to being overweight or obese (Cancer Research, July 2016). To be the best you can be, get yourself in shape – you'll feel better, look better and your self-confidence will soar.

People who date a lot are self-aware and project the best of themselves, in other words they make the most of themselves on a daily basis. Here's a bit of *Tough Love*, **you are not going to be asked out if you don't look like the person THEY want to meet**. Having a *"people have to take me as they find me"* attitude is all very well, but it isn't going to get you anywhere. You need to be and feel your best most of the time, because you have no idea when the opportunity to meet someone will present itself. Here's another bit of *Tough Love* **– you may hope Prince Charming is going to scour the land searching just for you**, but the truth is the dating market is crowded with people who look their best and talk with confidence. People who are always dating, bring a passion and enthusiasm to their outer selves, they glow because what they internally project shows. Even Miss Not-So-Fab can consistently be out on dates if she's packaged herself well. Whether you like it or not, always project the best of yourself.

Deciding to abandon her corset, has made a new woman out of Beatrice!

©Create Communication.2019

SECTION TWO

Who are you? It's a simple question but somewhere between 25 and 50, we become so many different people and wear so many varied hats we can lose sight of ourselves, our real selves. Self-awareness is a hard thing to acquire and maintain, because we're skilled at hiding the truth from ourselves. However, knowing ourselves truly, deeply and accurately matters a great deal because only when we're able to do that are we able to make reliable decisions, particularly when it comes to love. If I asked you to tell me all about yourself, what would you say? Many women say they're a Mother or they state their occupation, what they do for a living. But those labels are external, who are we really and why is this important when it comes to dating? Because if you don't know who you are, how are you going to find someone who will complement you.

Ability; Character & Emotions

Abilities: What can you do? And don't say *"nothing"*. You didn't get to this age without being able to do anything. One of the problems we have as women is we don't blow our own trumpet enough. We hide our abilities as if we are ashamed, but you have loads of skills and right now I want you to have a look at the abilities over the page and **tick the boxes** of the ones you can or can't do, I'm betting that you can do more than you think you can;

	I can do this	I can't do this
Organising: Can you organise your own and your children's calendars?		
Written communication: Can you express yourself clearly in writing?		
Numeracy: Can you add, multiply, and subtract?		
Driving: Can you drive a vehicle?		
Leadership: Do you lead your children or people at work and motivate them?		
Negotiating: Are you able to negotiate with family members, influence their actions? (particularly your kids)		
Time management: Do you manage your time effectively? Are you able to get things done in a day?		
Decision making: Can you decide the best course of action?		
Planning: Can you plan parties and other		

social occasions from beginning to end?		
Computing: Can you use the internet, type, use Word, Excel, PowerPoint?		
Initiative: Can you act on your own gut feelings and make decisions?		
Verbal communication: Can you talk to people?		
Creativity: Can you come up with new ideas and solutions?		

How did you do? I bet you have more yeses than no's! You may be even more surprised to know these skills which so many of us have perfected over the years as wives, daughters and mothers and rather take for granted, are precisely the skills called for by so many of the FTSE 100 companies. According to the University of Kent, skills, which you and I can do with our eyes closed are required by graduate recruits for the BBC, Microsoft and Target Jobs.
(https://www.kent.ac.uk/careers/sk/top-ten-skills.htm)

Here are a few more, tick them, feel confidence grow;

Extra Skills/Abilities- Can you do it?	YES	NO
Listening		
Cooking		
Sewing		
Decorating		
Gardening		
Tennis		
Golf		
Painting/craft		

Add your own further skills to this list. These are a solid foundation on which you can build when it comes to thinking who you are and what you can do.

Find Yourself Before You Find Love

Write down 5 words that describe you, e.g. fun, pragmatic, caring etc

1

2

3

4

5

When we describe ourselves, we're talking about personality which is what makes us different from one another. It's this set of individual traits that influence your interactions with and adaptations to the world in which you live. There are more than 20,000 personality trait adjectives in the English language, so analyzing your own, let alone someone else's can be a complex and confusing business.

As time and life move on, we can lose a sense of who we are, but although we think we've changed, the characteristics of our personality endure. We're still the same person we were last week, last month, last year, even though we may have had to adapt to challenges and problems.

If you look back at the 5 words you've used above, what you've actually written is your understanding of yourself. You may or may not be satisfied with that, but these words are an anchor. Our personality is relatively stable but our sense of ourselves changes all the time. For example, have you ever had your photo taken and as soon as you look at it you think – horrible, it makes me look fat/ugly/false. Those thoughts are as if you're taking a small hammer and chipping away at your self-esteem, and then you begin to wonder how others see you. Before you know it your sense of yourself is distorted.

Low self-esteem is extremely negative, and it tends to show itself to others. It creates an impression and rightly or wrongly tells others what they can expect from you. Fortunately, most of us have a mixed reaction to ourselves, for example you may feel good about your intellect, but less confident about talking to people you don't know. This just means you have high self-esteem in one area, but not in another, which is pretty normal. We live in a competitive world where we're regularly being compared in areas including finances, relationships, children, friendships, looks etc. Even if your self-esteem is sky high, it's sometimes harder to maintain than you'd like.

The fact is, you don't need to re-invent yourself to attract someone, why bother trying to be someone you're not when your personality is set the way it is. And even if you did carry it off at first, you certainly couldn't keep it up. You can't make yourself a gym babe if you hate exercise, you're never going to like it and you'll be throwing good money away. The best way to attract someone is to project the successful and thriving self-image that comes from high self-esteem.

So how do you raise your self-esteem. One strategy according to Brown and Smart (1991) is that you need to focus on areas of your life that are going well, even during a period when a lot is going wrong. People with high self-esteem will dwell on the positive and not the negative. For instance, you've been out on a great date and he says those magic words "*I'll call you*" and you wait and wait and wait. You may even text to nudge him in the right direction. You go from being ecstatic, to hoping the phone will ring, to heartbroken because it hasn't – all in a week!

If you've got low self-esteem, you'll by now be dwelling obsessively on an analysis. His failure to call you just confirms how you feel about yourself, unworthy and inadequate. What did you do or say that was wrong? Nothing is the answer so stop the way you're thinking right now. Change yourself into someone with high self-esteem. Remind yourself you're a great date, you have a ton of things going for you, a good sense of humour, you're a good daughter/parent/friend, you play a mean game of squash and the dog loves you! Just because you've had one bad experience doesn't mean you're not good enough, it means he wasn't good enough for *You!* In other words, the strategy used by high self-esteem people after a failure or a bad day is to remind themselves they're hugely successful in other areas and it's those on which they focus. Look at what you can do, not on what you can't.

Here's a little exercise you can do right now that will turn your dial from low self-esteem to high. And if you already have high self-esteem – well this will send you sky high. Make a list of the things going well in your life as well as what you're most proud of. Tuck it in your handbag. That way if you have a bad day and feel negativity sneaking in, you can take it out and review. High self-esteem is about saying 'Stuff you' to negativity and 'Stuff you' to those who bring you down.

To cut out and keep

10 Things I'm Proud Of such as: I can do 2 miles on the treadmill in under 20 minutes, I run my own business, I have a degree, I can hold down a full-time job, I cook a mean lasagne . . .

I'm proud that . . .

1

2

3

4

5

6

7

8

9

10

Nowadays we have so many different roles to fill it's not surprising the way we feel about ourselves, varies daily. The trick is to make the most of the good days, allow that self-esteem to rise high, and turn your back firmly on the bad days.

One thing I know for certain is that some form of exercise in the morning usually guarantees a better day. I should say at this point, I'm not a fitness fanatic but I do take care of my body and exercise regularly, whether a brisk walk, swimming or hitting the treadmill. You can do anything that takes your fancy, but for goodness sake do something. Studies show people who regularly exercise, benefit from a positive boost in mood and have lower rates of depression. This is because exercise causes chemicals called endorphins to be released and these interact with receptors in your brain, acting as an analgesic and reducing your perception of pain. They also trigger positive feelings, similar to the effect of morphine although these are far less likely to get you into trouble, unless it's you refusing to leave the gym!

Regular exercise will help to:

- Reduce stress, anxiety and depression
- Boost self-esteem.
- Increase energy levels.
- Improve sleep.
- Lower blood pressure.
- Reduce body fat.

And best news of all is you don't have to join an expensive gym you can:

- Take a brisk walk.
- Garden.
- Decorate.
- Jog.
- Do the housework especially the vacuuming.
- Swim.
- Play golf.

Notice that nowhere on that list is sitting watching TV.

Here's another piece of good news; while you're raising your self-esteem by exercising you're also getting out of the house - one of the most important things you can do. Shutting your door means you're shutting out the world and missing opportunities to meet someone new. Once you have higher self-esteem, you'll attract people with a similar philosophy. One of the problems in being over 40 is that there are more moaners around. They'll complain about their health, family, finances, weather, you name it they'll have a go. Don't get sucked into that. Distance yourself now. Moaners attract other moaners and believe me there are enough of them out there. It's not an attractive look and so off-putting. Align yourself with bubbly confident people who make you laugh and bring you joy. How do you open up your life? Well, to be very blunt, you need to go out. Going out will force you to meet other people even if it's only to say 'Hello' and in time those people will introduce you to other people. It's a continuous cycle. Learning something new or traveling is a great idea, it will give you something to talk about and open your eyes to other areas of life which previously may have been closed off.

Opening up your life brings all sorts of advantages, firstly it stops you being bored and secondly it forces you to embrace the fear of doing something outside your comfort zone. One of the best books I ever read was *Feel the Fear And Do It Anyway*®

by *Susan Jeffers*. I read it when I was 20 and have dipped in and out ever since. It's a bible book! The book's main concept is that everyone knows fear and to conquer it you have to tackle what you fear most. Fear paralyses you, fences you in and feeds on itself to make you even more fearful.

We all fear change whether it's being alone, failing at something or indeed sometimes we fear being successful. That little voice in our head spends more time telling us why we shouldn't do something than why we should. It's not surprising we don't take a lot of risks, after all we've all heard our parents shout 'Be careful! This taught us not to take a risk, 'Be careful, you might hurt yourself. Be careful you don't want to fall'. If only parents would say 'Go on - do it'.

One of the major changes you have to embrace is facing your fears and trying something new. It's the only way you're going to meet someone. Living in fear of going out and socialising means you're closing instead of opening up your world and therefore no-one can walk in.

Once you've decided to take the bull by the horns and open up - taking an evening course, a cookery class, learning to salsa – you'll see yourself differently. The first time you do anything new is always difficult, but the second time is a piece of cake. I remember the first time I decided to go Ceroc dancing. I was 36, left my two children with a babysitter, drove to the village hall and sat in my car for ages watching people go in and hearing the music. Eventually I got out and walked in. No-one turned and stared at me, someone found me a partner ready for the lesson and for the next hour I danced. Then I got back in my car and went home. Did any harm come to me? Of course not. Did I feel proud of myself? You bet your bottom dollar I did. I went back time and again and found a whole new group of friends that would become a great support group to each other.

Change and trying new things isn't easy, it takes courage to decide you need to do something. There are all sorts of obstacles, both real and imagined. Don't let this deter you, opening up your life, means you're starting to take control. The more in control you feel, the more confident you'll be and the more you'll attract others.

More **Tough Love; if you do nothing you'll get nowhere**. You can read this book over and over but if you don't take action nothing will happen. If you don't want to be in the same place in 6 months you have to do something to make your life different. Do it now!

Being over 40 and looking for love means you need a healthy social life. Not only does this increase your chances of meeting someone but having a great set of friends gives you a support system and stops you being bored. Most people go to work, come home, deal with kids/pets/parents, eat, watch tv, sleep and then repeat. You can change that by creating a good social life, which is easier than ever on the internet where every type of activity/club/course is posted daily.

Find something that's of interest to you and you'll find like-minded people. I'd recommend *www.meetup.com*. They cover just about every city and town and there's a plethora of social activities to choose from. I recently went to a *Learn about Wine* meet up and had a great time. There were about 40 people of all different ages and of course we all ended up talking, we'd shared the experience (and the wine!). Meetup groups meet regularly and the more you go, the more likely you are to meet someone, plus you're expanding your own interests and knowledge.

Liking yourself and enjoying your own company is crucial, how can you expect anyone else to enjoy it, if you don't? What is it about you that makes you special? Don't just shrug your shoulders and say you don't know, you need to think about what you can do, what good qualities you have, what skills, what knowledge and what experience you have. It's funny, but we all think we don't have or know a lot, but recently I was applying for a new job and had to fill out an extensive application form, matching my skills to the person specification form. I found that not only could I match the skills but could easily provide evidence where I had used those skills in the past.

Remember you're a whole person, not half a person looking for the *other half*; you have skills and knowledge that have taken years to accumulate which means dating at forty can be more rewarding than dating in your twenties. You have more experience, you've probably travelled more, you may have even been through the whole marriage palaver, which makes you a far more interesting and intriguing person – a person who can hold thought-provoking conversations and debates.

Know who you are. Don't put yourself last, put yourself first. Many of us women were taught to put others first, and if you have children you may think you come lower down in the pecking order. The consequence of that is feeling unworthy, under-valued and sometimes resentful. You need to put yourself first at times, attend to yourself and fill yourself with joy. You are responsible for your own happiness and as soon as you're genuinely happy and joyful, people will flock towards you.

Dating isn't going to make you happy, only you can make yourself happy. If you think you can meet someone to do it for you, you're in for a disappointment. Your date is only there to add more happiness and to share in yours. Nothing more. Never put the responsibility of your happiness on someone else – the risk is too great.

What makes you happy? Each row of this chart represents different areas of your life: family, education, health, social life, work and money. You can substitute these with other things if you want. Look at the segments and fill them in, up to the point where you feel it fits your happiness. For example, if you are only 50% happy with your health, fill in the health segment half way starting from number one. On the other hand, you may be 90% happy with your work, so that row almost to the end. Have a look at the worked example and then fill in your own.

	1	2	3	4	5	6	7	8	9	10
Family Relationships	■	■	■	■	■	■	■			
Education	■	■	■	■						
Health	■	■	■	■	■	■	■			
Social life	■	■	■	■	■	■	■	■		
work	■	■	■	■	■					
Money	■	■	■	■	■	■	■			

	1	2	3	4	5	6	7	8	9	10
Family Relationships										
Education										
Health										
Social life										
Work										
Money										

In an ideal world, the chart should have every segment filled to 100%, but of course that's never going to happen because we live on planet Earth and not on planet Hollywood Movie Land. There are going to be times when some pieces of the pie are fuller than others, but it's the ones that are lowest you need to focus on. If you're happy with a segment being at 30% then that's fine, if not, do something about it. For example, I wasn't happy about my general knowledge being low, I found it intimidating to talk to guys about politics and news, so I decided I'd read a good newspaper every day for a week and see if that increased my conversational skills - and you know what, it did. Soon I found I was genuinely interested in political affairs that affected me and with that interest, I became more interesting to others. A friend of mine, Laura, found her low segment was work, so she started looking for other jobs, but soon realised it wasn't a different job she needed, but a whole new way of working. She decided she wanted to do something completely different. She took an evening class, gained a florist qualification and set up her own part-time business. Eventually she gave up her day job and now works full-time from home creating silk flower arrangements.

Being happy with yourself is something most of us haven't thought about in a long while but thinking what actions you can take to make yourself happy, is a powerful tool. Once you're happy, finding someone will be easy, because your happiness will colour every single aspect of your life and it really is in your control.

I understand it's not possible to be happy if you are depressed but there's a clear distinction between feeling low and suffering an actual depressive illness, where professional help is usually needed. If you're feeling low, try hard to address it and accept nobody is happy all the time, there are always things that get us down. Continued unhappiness leads to bitterness which is reflected outwardly and that won't attract anyone.

"Often, it's not about becoming a new person, but becoming the person you were meant to be, and already are, but don't know how to be."

Heath L. Buckmaster. Box of Hair: A Fairy Tale

SECTION 3

Finding the elusive male

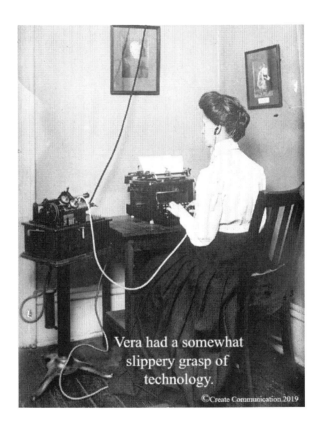

Vera had a somewhat slippery grasp of technology.

©Create Communication.2019

The Internet and why online apps rarely work for the over 40s:
Tinder has approximately 50 million users* so with that statistic
you would think there must be one, just one person out there
that you could date. But holy moly there isn't. In fact, when I
mention dating apps or any type of online dating sites to my

clients, they all roll their eyes to heaven and launch into a torrid of problems they have encountered, and yet a third of modern marriage have started with an online date.

So, why is it that it's a hit or miss affair? Many reasons, from the fact that its all to do with the way you look or at least are photogenic, to the age demographic but I think it's a bit more than that, people in their 40s, 50s and 60s are looking for romance, a bit of the romance they had when they were younger or at least dreamed of and it is true to say that these apps sell romance in their advertising but what they really do is introducing people. That's it, they introduce people and just because people are using websites doesn't meant they are meeting people for long term love and happiness, it simply means they are using them. Can you see the issue here?

Most of us go on to these apps full of hope and excitement. You dream of the possibilities because you have invested time in the initial process like filling in a questionnaire (one online dating website's questionnaire took me three hours to do!), finding photos, thinking of something funny to write. Before you know it, your profile is posted, you become a bubbling mix of excitement and nerves and low and behold you open the app and you are "matched" with people who live near you and seem to have the same values as you. How then, you may ask yourself, have you never met these people before? Now to be fair to dating apps you could never really meet these people before because it would be like finding a needle in a haystack. Before apps you would go out on a Saturday night and a) try to pluck up the courage to meet someone and b) hope that after taking the plunge to talk to someone that they have something in common with you. Nowadays that's taken away from you. You can look online and be "introduced" to someone who does want to talk and according to the magic of the algorithm you will have something in common. BUT and here's the bit of **Tough Love, you are getting together with a total stranger – how scary is that?**

Generally speaking before online dating we went out with people we met in school, work or our friends knew them, or as in a lot of communities your guy would be a friend of a brother whose sister you knew. Most people married someone who lived within a mile of each other.

Of course, the main problem with online dating especially when you are 40 plus is the lying and let's face it we all do it. Suddenly we are slightly younger, thinner, taller. Come on, don't tell me you haven't exaggerated the truth but so what, when you do meet that person does it really matter if the sparks fly? No, but what it does do is creates a level of suspicion if they or even you can lie about that then what else is a lie. The problems that we have in real-life will creep up on us on our online life.

So why do apps rarely work for people who are in their 40s, 50s and 60s because we are old romantics who are looking for love not just to be introduced to a total stranger who wants to message forever and not actually meet up; because the app itself constantly pulls you back into searching and unless you have great restraint you will always think there could be someone else out there that's fitter, younger, taller etc and if you are thinking that then so are they; and the main problem is that the more months you spend on these apps meeting no-one the more money the apps are making and that, is the bottom line.

If, on the other hand, you do decide to go down the internet dating route, make sure you put up a great picture, not just a good picture, but your best. According to eHarmony advice, photos are what matters most to men when it comes to your online dating profile. They can drastically increase your chances of getting more communication and dates. Their research shows people who uploaded 4 or more photos received the most communication from their matches. Looking at their data shows that 4 photos gets you 80% more communication and 10, 90%. Personally, I wouldn't overload it, I think 4 – 5 is great. They recommend a mixture of landscape and portrait photos and ones where you are doing something like traveling on a ski-lift or walking in the woods. Close-ups funnily enough get very little interest. Whatever you upload, make sure it is a clear, good quality photo and always remember to smile. A study by Tracy and Beall (2011) found that men were most attracted to women displaying happiness. Seems pretty obvious doesn't it, but there are many photos up there where the person looks seriously somber. Perhaps they think it's sexy, I'm not so sure.

To save time, you could narrow your search to a small location or a certain set of *must have* features. Only talk to those who make the list. When communicating keep the initial online conversation focused on finding out the basics, then set up an actual date. Don't do long introductory emails they may be counter-productive and off-putting. I would also add you shouldn't use your *must haves* as a shield. Just because someone doesn't fit the spec perfectly, doesn't mean he isn't worth a date, keep in mind, as we grow older we may need to shift our expectations. Also, always meet in a public place. Never get him to pick you up or take you home until you are really sure. And remember, matchmaking sites are a business, they're not there to spread the love, they're in it to make money so pick your site well.

Build your own network:

Edna's social circle was not quite as lively as she might have hoped!
©Create Communication 2019

The best way is to be introduced to someone, now before you cry *"but that's the problem, I don't know anyone who can introduce me,"* I want to show you a way in which you can expand your network. When I say networking I mean really make it a task in which you can expand the people you know because the more people you know the more opportunities you have of meeting someone.

We all have friends even if its just one, we keep the same friends who have similar interests because that's what makes them friends. However, unless your friends can introduce you to someone then you definitely need to expand your network. Networking to meet someone takes on the same premise of networking for business. According to Robbie Kellman Baxter of Linkedin Learning, you need to have 7 types of people in your network in order to be successful in business networking and I would say that the same needs to happen in your social life network. By expanding your social circle through networking, you will be extending your reach and the opportunity to meet others including the one that will introduce you to the new guy in your life.

So here are the 7 types of people you need:

1. Current Friends, these are people you already know.
2. People you could be friendly with, for example a friend of a friend or someone you just met whilst walking the dog.
3. Someone you look up to, who gives you advice like a family member.
4. Old friends, who you don't see that often but keep in touch with once a year at Christmas
5. People who know a lot of people. These are people who in one shape or another know a lot of people, they are connectors, they go to parties/lunches or dinners. These are the people who could invite you to a place you wouldn't normally get an invite to.

6. People who you call upon to help you or do provide a service for you for example your hairdresser, manicurist, professional stylist. These types of people meet lots of people every day, they hear their stories and you want them to put you in touch with who they meet if they are suitable.

7. People who are newly on their own, for example someone who has just got divorced or widowed. These people will be more than eager to meet up because they are lost and in a whole new world, but they also know people so not only do you gain a new friend also access to their social group.

Make a list of these types of people and start to reach out to them. Some people you will invite for a coffee and some you will might just send a card, you need to start regularly being in touch. If you are not in their mind then you won't get the invitation or introduction. Networking with these people who you should have on your list will help you to:

- Connect you to the elusive male
- Connect you to someone who knows the elusive male
- Give you a tip on where to meet the elusive male
- Get you invited to an event to meet that elusive male.

As you tap into people in your network so your network will

simultaneously grow. I would encourage you that if anyone in your network invites you somewhere even if you think it's a dead loss just go, you just never know. Here's what happened to me, when I was first single after being in a marriage for 8 years, I expanded my network by joining a Ceroc dance club. I learnt to dance and by default Ceroc is a dance where you have to do it with a male lead. So, here I was dancing with these guys who in turn introduced me to other women. Now, I have to say at this point that everyone in this group was in their 20s and I was very near to my 40s with two children. However, that did not deter me. They had a fabulous social life mainly around the dancing scene and they would invite me along. One evening over the Christmas period they invited me to a "mulled wine and mince pie evening". It was as dull as it sounds and after an hour, I left with one other woman to go to see if we could get a drink at a bar to nurse our sorrows of having spent the whole evening in dullness. The bar was about to take the last orders when a guy and his friend approached me and my friend. We chatted over a drink, the bar closed, we chatted outside. I said "goodbye", he said "can I call you?", we spent the next 14 years of our lives together. That's the power of growing your network.

The next step is to nurture your network, it's a bit like a garden, you tend to the soil, put in the seeds and in order to get the flowers you need to water, pick off bugs and feed. Your network is the same. Make a list, make contact, take some of them out for a coffee or lunch, introduce some people to others and in time you will see the results because you will know so many people that eventually you will not only meet the elusive male but also you will have a great and different social life.

Places to meet

Bars/Pubs/Clubs: Noisy, but sociable. People go to pubs to meet others, but while men mainly go to meet male friends, chat and drink, women go to see their friends and meet someone. So, that's an issue, and it is awkward to meet anyone in a bar when you're over 40 you can't just smile and hope a guys will come over, you don't know who's single and who isn't.

At work: Whether you work full or part time you spend a great many hours there and this can sometimes be a meeting people forum. Of course, work is what you're there for, but it's often an opportunity to meet or talk to all types of people from different areas of the country. There always has been and always will be a certain amount of office flirting, especially among the young. There are also office affairs, supposedly secret, but in fact general knowledge.

Meeting someone who is free, however, is common in an office environment no matter what your age. A word of warning though, over the age of 40 you don't want to look like a giggly 20 year old. A younger girl can get away with it and if things don't work out can generally leave and get another job. At 40 plus, this may not be so easy, you might be working because you have children and this company lets you work around school holidays or might be conveniently local. Finding another job which suits as well, might not be so simple. If you do see someone at work who happens to be single, my advice would be easy does it, make sure he's interested before you embark on even a small amount of flirting. Don't be an embarrassment to you, him or the company. However, once past these possible pitfalls, meeting regularly at work means you have a reason to converse "The coffee machine's broken down again" type of conversation which can lead to "Do you fancy going out for a coffee?" But beware nowadays, any kind of flirting may be misconstrued and interpreted as sexual harassment. So, always be aware of yourself at work. All is not as clear cut as it once was.

The Matchmaker: It sounds old-fashioned, but in the days of having to do-it-yourself on the internet dating sites, having a matchmaker can take the stress out of dating. A good personal matchmaker will meet and get to know you. Only at that point would she offer you a date she believes will suit you. The benefit is you know you will have something in common with the person to whom you're introduced and that your expectations are being managed, obviously this isn't the case with online dating. Matchmakers aren't cheap but will introduce you to someone you'll get on with and depending on the terms of your agreement with them, will keep on introducing you, until you find someone you think you want a long-term relationship with.

There are two ways of being on a Matchmaker's books, firstly there are the network clients. These are people who normally join for free. They are people who will be available for dating a client who has paid. They may or may not have actually met the Matchmaker, but they would have filled out a lengthy form giving full details about themselves. Secondly, there are the clients who have paid. These are the people the Matchmaker is actually working for. This type of client has paid anywhere between £1000 or £25,000 upwards for a number of matches over a 6 – 12 month period. Some Matchmakers have an age limit on the women they will take on to their books for free, so it's best to give them a call.

Meetup.com: This is a way of getting involved with activities you enjoy without creating the pressure normally associated with dating groups. The website, www.meetup.com offers groups within your area with different interests for example, the *Badminton Player Group*, *Entrepreneur Network*, *Walkers Group*, *Pub Group* and even the *London Shyness Social Group*.

You can join a group knowing you'll meet someone with a common interest and better still, in your local area. Even if you don't meet anyone there you may make some great new friends who could introduce you to someone. Groups meet regularly, you don't have to go to every single one, go to those you have time for. If you've made a list of the type of person you want to meet, go to groups you think that person is more likely to go to. Sign up to the hiking group if you want to meet the outdoor type. There are also a lot of women's groups which are great for meeting people and increasing your circle of friends.

Art Galleries and Museums: Go to one of the exhibitions, study a John Sargent or a Monet and see who stands next to you or go stand next to a man who catches your eye! I recently went to an exhibition at the Royal Academy, it was full of gorgeous men. Many galleries/museums also have evening events, either talks or socials. Worth going if you want to meet a like-minded person.

The Park: Full of divorced dads with kids or men who like to exercise/cycle. Start running in the park in the mornings (Parkrun is free and meets across the country) or join the outdoor boot camp. My single friend Phillipa joined an outdoor training boot camp held in her local park, she found the main core of regulars go for coffee after the class and are genuinely friendly – it gave her Sunday mornings a whole new look.

The Porsche Garage (or any other sport car showroom): Full of men who like to look at the newest models. Go and have a look at the cars as if you might be buying. Ask the guy what he thinks of it – it's a winner every time. Get to know the sales person and ask them to put you on the list for the event when a new car is bought out. This is an exclusive champagne evening showing the new car and is attended by men, lots of them.

Evening Classes: opt for business courses, languages, stock-market analysis or art. *Crocheting* might be fun, it's unlikely it will get you a man!

Church/Synagogue/Mosque: high days and holy days draw the biggest crowd. If you're a regular attender, you'll soon get to know the congregation and someone will either catch your eye or some kind person will introduce you to another. Many temples hold social events, quizzes and dinners. Long-term relationships often start off by meeting in a religious setting, these couples tend to share a spiritual connection and therefore they will be not only connected as a couple but supported by the community.

Get A Dog: Possibly the number one way to meet someone. Obviously, a dog is for life, not just for dating, so think carefully, although the great advantage is that even if the right man doesn't materialize, there will always be someone who unconditionally adores you, always wants a cuddle and won't answer you back!

Accept the Blind Date: Let your friends set you up, It doesn't have to be a meaningful date, it's just going out. Going to the cinema on a mid-week blind date means at least you get to see a movie on a Wednesday night, instead of watching TV or doing the ironing. Take it lightly. Just going out is important, it doesn't mean you're desperate, it means you're open to others and it will get you back in the swing of things.

Tennis: If you don't play, learn. It's the most sociable sport ever. According to Sport England, there are two age groups who regularly play tennis, those that are younger than 20 and those that are 40 plus. Not only is it great for getting fit and staying healthy, it's a sport where you have to team up with someone else to play, and at the end of the match you can go for coffee and meet others who are single and want to play.

With all the above you have to make an effort. You can go to any event or gathering and not meet anyone, but you certainly won't if you don't go. And talking is the key. It doesn't matter if the other person makes an excuse after a few minutes and walks away, who cares. Making contact with someone you don't know is scary, but it may lead to something. It takes time and effort to network, make sure you do something at least once a month, it's a numbers game at the end of the day.

SECTION 4

HELP, I HAVE KIDS -HELP, HE HAS KIDS!

I've got kids! Let's talk about dating men with children, and how to involve them with yours. When I was a child/ teenager, one of my favourite television shows was The Brady Bunch. Two widowed people married and had 6 children between them. They were always out on wonderful adventures and of course they all loved each other – only in America! Dating when you both have children can be tricky but also can have advantages because you both have a) something in common and b) are going through similar times in your lives. You both understand that kids come first, which people who don't have children can't but you can both feel confused and pulled in several directions by different demands.

Dating at over forty, is not going to put you in line for men who want to have a large family, our biological clock has tocked. Besides, dealing with a baby at 45 is exhausting and personally I'd rather be sitting by a pool than changing a nappy or negotiating with a toddler. However, the good news is that 74% of respondents to the "State of Dating in America Report" written by Elyse Romano, showed individuals would probably or definitely marry someone

Mother said to sprinkle the rose petals. She didn't say not to sprinkle drawing pins!

©Create Communication.2019

with children from a previous relationship. Single parents who are worried that their childless dates would never want to take on a step-parent role can relax. Apparently, they are far more open to the idea than one may think.

The other great thing about dating a man with children is he already knows what family life is about and can't wait to get back into it. Of all the men there are out there, this is the one type who really wants to be married again. Fact: divorced men with children get married quicker than those without. Another great thing about this type of man is he has already owned a house and will either have another one on his own or something he is renting. If you do find he is back living with his Ma or Pa, you can bet your bottom dollar it won't be long before he wants to get out and buy again. Men with children have experience of life which younger men don't. They've been up at the crack of dawn feeding a baby and have definitely changed a nappy or two. It all adds to their character. You can see by the way he interacts with his children, what kind of man he is and how he shows his feelings.

Many people will often filter out single dads in their internet searches. Perhaps they don't want to get involved with guys who have "baggage" but remember this, it's the person you want to be involved with. Don't filter those men out, think wider than that.

Personally, I had two small children when I met my long-term partner, he didn't have children and I thought that might put him off me, however he decided to go with the flow and we had great times together. At forty and beyond, both men and women know that neither of you are without risks or baggage and if you put a filter on people who have kids you could be missing out on a great relationship.

Introducing a man to your kids

Get him to know you first, the kids later. Also, you don't need to blurt out within in the first 5 minutes of meeting that you have a family. It isn't necessary. Getting to know someone means you need to get to know each other's personality. You are you, not someone's mother, you become you again and that's refreshing. After about a couple of dates I did tell him I had children. I didn't have anything to worry about, he had guessed. Of course, looking back, he didn't have to be a genius to know. I lived in a family house with a garden, had a family car (large enough for weekly shopping, a buggy and school PE kit), only worked part-time, he'd have had to be blind not to know. But, I was holding back. One thing I learned is you don't spill the beans your life too fast. Let him be the one to probe. Just be casual, you don't need to have a serious talk about your children, just mention them, I think I said something like "Can't meet on Sunday, it's my son's birthday". That was it, job done.

The other thing I learned was not to make things complicated, I never bored him with my ex- husband's weekend rights or my babysitter arrangements, your date doesn't want to know, doesn't need to know. Your date needs to get to know you and not the complicated parts of your life involving your ex-husband, court dates and maintenance payments. You need a new man to get to know you, your personality and your best side. Life on your own with children is hard, it can be stressful. I found dealing with my ex-husband, money and kids demands almost put me on the edge of the cliff, praying for a gust of wind. However, having a person who takes you out of that life and wants to be part of the new you, is, in itself therapy. I never regretted my children going to my ex- husband for the weekend, why would I? It was a rest. I could catch up on my housework, go out for coffee, shop, have dinner with my date without having to worry about time. Bloody brilliant. One Monday morning I took my children to primary school and in the playground a yummy mummy came up to me to compliment me on how well I looked. I told her I had read the entire Sunday paper and gone out for lunch with my new man, I can't begin to tell you how wonderful that felt!

When I say introduce your date to your children slowly, I say this because you need to make sure you want to introduce this person. Wait until you're sure your date is going to be a long-term man before involving him. This is for your children's sake as well as yours. Your children don't need to meet every Tom, Dick or Harry. Children are not particularly subtle, if they have met someone you were dating before, even if only for a couple of weeks, you don't want them telling your new man, how much they liked/hated them. I found it best to introduce a date in a public arena and that isn't around a table in a restaurant. You really want to be out doing something. If you have young children I recommend a trip to the zoo, a park or a museum. The kids have plenty to look at and do and it takes the pressure off you and him. For older children or teenagers, you could do go-karting, tennis, sledging (if there's snow!) or a theme park. Chances are teenagers can be a bit stroppy and certainly don't like hanging out with anyone over the age of 25 anyway, so it may not be easy, but if they will go out with you and your date for a couple of hours, make it fun.

The reason I advise against a restaurant is there may be awkward silences you're desperate to fill. Teenagers can be non-communicative, surviving on two or three words, yes, no and a grunt (which frankly could mean anything). This can be awkward for any parent who has bragged how wonderfully sociable her children are, remember any statement can come back and slap you in the face. Kids become silent for the first time ever, you become a nervous chatterbox, talk complete rubbish and laugh like a demented hyena. Even your children will be looking at you like you're some kind of nut. Don't do it. Better to take them to a fast food outlet after an activity where you've all had fun, than a sit-down 3 courses where every single one of you is waiting for a chance to bolt out the door.

Take the time to get to know his children

Kids are strange creatures, one minute they love you and the next they're having a temper tantrum. His kids might not like you at first and vice versa. Be prepared. You're in it for the long haul not the quick step. Always remember, you and your man are the adults and they are the children, no matter what their age. I've known children of 35 have the *great opinion* about whether their mother should be dating or not. Give me a break! One of the things to bear in mind is you can't force a relationship, it takes time. You need to all get to know each other and spend a little time together first before spending a lot of time. A weekend might seem a good idea, but rarely is, you'll all be running for the hills after an hour or two. It's better to build brick by brick.

Will the real mum or dad stand up?

Blood is thicker than water and never is that truer than when other mums or dads are involved. You need to set your roles; your kids already have a father (no matter what you think of him) and his kids already have a mother (same applies). Children may feel disloyal if they like you or him. Both of you need to build trust with the kids and reassure them no-one is being replaced. A word of advice, no matter what whining goes on about the other's ex, never get involved yourself, you will always come off worst. His kids might say something bad about their mother, but they will think they have the right, you do not and it can come back and bite you in the bum when you least expect it.

There is enough love to go around

You can love your own children, his children and him. Obviously each one is a different love, but the more you put out there, the more will come back. You may not always say or do the right thing, and you will make mistakes but the thing most of us remember is how someone makes us feel and if you give, share and love you can't go wrong.

My children don't want me to date, but I want to, how do I handle this?

As much as you love your children, they live in their own universe which consists of them first and foremost, their needs, their wants and anything else to do with them. You're probably on the periphery. You're there for them, not the other way round, so the fact you might want to go out and, shock horror meet someone can be really alien to them. Obviously, it depends on your children's age, but I tend to find teenagers particularly difficult. They will be *ill* just as you're walking out the door or they'll want an in-depth conversation with you about the universe as you're rushing around trying to find your keys. They're pretty good at delaying tactics.

You give a lot to your kids, in fact more than a lot and they have friends so why can't you? Explain you're just finding other friends so you can go out when they are with their friends. When I first dated, I kept in the back of my mind that eventually my kids would grow up and leave home and I wanted and needed to have my own group of friends and even a boyfriend. I kept it firmly in my mind because guess what, my kids are now young men and believe me don't give much thought to what I'm doing on a Saturday night so long as I've left food in the fridge and jeans washed and hanging in their wardrobe! Thank goodness I took time to expand my interests and find someone I could go out or sit in with on a Saturday night.

My children are keen for me to meet someone

Great, what you waiting for? Go out, join groups, you have their permission and now you just need to have fun. For many of us over 50, our children already have lives of their own and therefore don't need you so much if at all. This can be extremely daunting at first and perhaps hard to let go of the children you've nurtured. However, once they're older, at university or even moved out, your life is going to be different. It is your duty to go out and make a life for yourself, so your kids don't have to worry about you. Meeting someone once your children are adults increases your chances of meeting someone designed just for you. You don't need to make sure they fully love your kids, you don't need to plan days out so they can connect. This guy is for you. Obviously, it's much better if everyone gets on, but if your kids aren't living at home, or are not around at the weekend, you have in a way returned to your twenties when all you had to think about was you.

SECTION FIVE

QUESTIONS, WORRIES & SITUATIONS

Daphne feels getting back to nature could work wonders for her worries.

©Create Communication 2019

Why don't men approach me?

It's a sad fact that while some women have men approaching them, that's never been my own experience. In fact, whenever I watch a film and the handsome guy just happens to stand next to the girl and says something funny, I actually laugh out loud. I'm far more likely to get the guy who spills the coffee - and probably over me. It's not even that I'm unfriendly or unattractive but out of 100% of available men, a small minority will never approach anyone ever while another small minority of men will approach anyone, who breathes and is wearing a skirt.

Therefore of all the men left who would like to approach you the opportunity just isn't there. They usually won't approach if you're with someone else (male or female), they won't approach if you look as if you're busy, they won't approach if you're in a crowd. In fact, there are 1001 reasons why they won't approach you. So, it's up to you to make the opportunity. Step away from the crowd you are in and smile. If you're brave enough to mouth "Hi," even better. If it sounds like something from a romcom movie, don't worry, after all, movies are based on real life.

Smiling is probably the singular most important thing you can do to increase your chances. Anyone who's happy is going to attract someone. If you don't smile, you come across as standoffish and it's all downhill from there. Men take a smile as a signal and although it isn't guaranteed he'll come over, you have far more of a chance than if you gave him a glare or a stare. Talking of which, there's a world of difference between catching his eye or staring as if you're "Chucky", weighing him up for your next meal. Laughing, smiling and having fun gives an air of confidence and as I've said, confidence is the sexiest attribute a woman can have. Being sure of yourself, knowing yourself and your positive attitude will make you glow. They won't be able to resist!

Getting the conversation started

When I say tell your date something about yourself, I don't mean taking over the conversation and not letting your date get a word in edgeways, but simply showing who you are and being interesting. Although you shouldn't forget a quote from Lady Astor who once declared, "Anyone can get a man with the one simple sentence; Tell me more about yourself."

The simplest thing to measure in a successful meeting/date is who's doing the talking. If you're talking more than your date, the chances of success are lower. This may be a sweeping statement but when I was a psychology student, I learned questions were powerful behaviours because they controlled listener's attention. Verbal behaviour can broadly be divided into two – the givers and the seekers. Think back to schooldays, when the teacher was giving information, you could let your mind wander, but you got into trouble when she started to ask questions. We learn from an early age to pay more attention to seeking behaviours than to giving ones, which is why questioning controls attention because it requires response.

However, it's not just enough to question, you need to listen. Remember what he tells you, so you can ask him about it next time you see him. Listening is a woman's best weapon - it just about takes the place of a gorgeous face or body. Men love to talk, and they'll love you for listening.

I want to flirt but can't remember how!

Flirting, one of the joys of life. Flirting bridges the gap between knowing we like someone and letting them know too. Flirting is an easy way to convey what particular elements we like. It's flattering, everyone wants to know what someone else likes about them. You could easily just say "You look nice in that jumper." Flirting doesn't have to be false or manipulative, it is in fact a pleasure to convey to another person what you find attractive about them. Make a flirtatious remark about their appearance and/or character and you won't go far wrong. Hopefully they'll reciprocate and that's a real ego boost.

Can you lose the touch? Twenty years of cooking, cleaning and running the kids around means flirting is probably the last thing you've been worried about brushing up on. Many dates when you are over 40, don't consist of any type of flirting it's more a question of telling your life story to one another and getting out of there. Personally, I like flirting, a bit of banter, touching the arm or hand of someone when you talk is lovely. The problem is some men and women take a chat over a drink to be a bit like an interview. Even where you sit is important. If you can sit up on bar stools that's great, because you have to turn to face each other whilst sitting at a table means although you're facing, you have to reach over the table to touch. What happens if the other person pulls away suddenly? It's embarrassing. You're left hanging half-way across the table, reaching out to nothing because their hands are now very firmly in their lap or worse, at the back of their head.

So where to begin? First with eye contact, look into their eyes. This is not staring, nor is it a first-to- blink contest, but simply gazing at the other person will bring out your flirtatious nature.

Secondly, smile and not just with your mouth, a genuine smile will light up your eyes and of course those eyes are gazing at your date. A smile can light up a room, it gives you confidence, you will be radiant and glowing and there's nothing more attractive.

When you are gazing and smiling you will find your body moves naturally and if your partner is feeling the same he will unconsciously replicate your movement.

What to say? Well, steer clear of politics, religion or children. Complimenting is always a good place to start. I normally start with what they're wearing "Nice shirt", or talk about where you are, "This is nice, I've always wanted to come here" – these little compliments go a long way, less is more really. If you say the place is nice the guy interprets that as his choice is a good one, he will take full credit for it, believe me, as he will if you say the food is great, he'll be as chuffed as if he'd knocked it up himself.

By now you should be in close proximity, hopefully only a few inches apart, not yelling across the table. Find some common ground, keep it light, no heavy personal stuff. He doesn't need to know how bitter your divorce was, how many times you went to court or how your mother is feeling. Avoid debates, criticisms and certainly no complaints. In fact, if your date starts to complain then get the hell out of there, it will be a constant rant of a relationship with nothing being right.

Break the touch barrier by lightly touching their arm or their hand, just gently. This suggests you like them and are comfortable with yourself and the moment. It will come naturally, don't force it.

Like all things keep it short and sweet. Get them wanting more. When you flirt you are playing the Law of Attraction, flirting is a shift in the energy field and for a fleeting moment it can leave a mark that carries sustainable results. Every moment of flirting brings a chance to connect to one another.

Wrap up the date with a smile and just say "Great to see you, hope to see you again". Let them want to take your number, let them want to see you again. Play the game, you have to let them chase you until you decide you want to be caught!

Why are you attracted to some people and not to others, and why is it the people you're attracted to don't fancy you?

Attraction is what makes one person feel positively about another, it means wanting to know and spend time with that person. The more attractive you are the more positively people will judge you (Langlois et al 2000). In Langlois meta-analysis she concludes that although beauty is more than skin deep, those who are attractive tend to exhibit more positive behaviours and traits. Perhaps this is because attractive people are treated better in the world than unattractive people and therefore we are attracted to people who not only look good but of the positive attitude the give out.

We also like people who are similar to us and therefore we go for people who we look positively at. We're also attracted to people who think in the same way, because it reinforces what we already think. For example, if you say you think all cars should be electric and the other person agrees, it reinforces your opinion, you therefore feel happier and as a consequence the reinforcer is more attractive.

We tend to be attracted to people with the same social background, interests and sociability because once again it reinforces our own personality and traits. However, what makes someone more attractive is the cost/reward. This may make socialising seem like a business deal, but it's instinctive to seek to obtain, preserve or exchange things of value with others and to bargain over what we're prepared to give in exchange for what we get. We aim to minimise cost and maximise reward.

When we're attracted to someone we automatically check potential cost and reward, comparing those with other relationships that might be available. Although this may sound devious, it's what we humans do. So, when you go out with someone you'll define the level of attraction depending on the reward, for example: did you have a nice time? Could you see yourself developing a relationship? Then you subtract cost. Did you have to pay anything towards the date? How difficult were the meeting arrangements? Did the way he was dressed make a good first impression?

Your opinion (and his) will be swayed by how these elements and others such as comparison with other dates, weigh up, and whether one outbalances the other. Whatever we want in physical attraction there's always something else going on. On a date, you don't know who you're being compared to or whether the cost is too high for him. You may have a great time and be convinced you are compatible, yet your date doesn't call again. Don't take this personally, rather look on it as a lucky escape, because you don't want to be someone who will *do*, until someone better comes along. Think about it as just another experience until someone whose rewards outweigh costs comes along.

What if the only man I'm attracted to is married?

You only have to listen to your divorced friends to find out some of them have been cheated on by their ex-husbands, it therefore won't come as a shock to you to know that some men like to be married with all the trimmings and have a girlfriend on the side. It may be that you don't mind meeting a married man, however apart from moral reasons there are numerous practical problems such as he can't see you on a Saturday night or stay over when he does see you. When you are young and single, married men might be a thrill, they are probably some of the most loving, sexually accomplished men you will ever meet, and better still you can use them for dinner and sex, then boot them out of your flat and they will still come back for more.

But you're no longer 20, and you know more now than you did then. Married men don't get a divorce, they are though usually divorced by their wives when they get found out. I would venture a rough guess that only a very few actually leave wives to marry the girlfriend they are having an affair with. Unsurprisingly, most women don't generally bring up in conversation the fact that they got together with their husband when they were having an affair behind his wife's back. Furthermore, men who have been unfaithful, rarely marry their current girlfriend and instead usually end up marrying someone new. Somebody, who hasn't been involved in that "not so secret part of his life." Why? Because, if he has children, he doesn't want to bring that part of his life into theirs, they will hate that mistress forever because of what she did to their lovely mother.

Married men are not available to go to weddings, barmitzvahs or funerals; office parties are out, sitting with your family at Christmas isn't going to happen and two-week holidays are a complete no-no. They also continue to sleep with their wives, even when they deny it. Sex is sex at the end of the day.

A married man who wants to embark on an affair, has plenty of chances, but he doesn't have an affair for the same reasons as you might. You might want someone loving, which he will be, whilst not having any full-time demands made on you. That is what you'll get, but not for the reasons you think. He will be loving because a heavy love affair is good for his ego and he might be bored with his long-term married relationship. He won't demand total love and commitment, that's not want he wants, why would he if he can't give it himself?

He might well love you and assure you, you'll be together, but I'm afraid 9 times out of 10 he can't say *when* that will be. Unless you've been given an actual date, time and location, the sentence "I love you and we will be together on such and such a date." Then doesn't mean a thing. Dating a married man means you have to wait for him and his wife to separate and this deadline may be a moveable thing There will never be a good time, December will be too near Christmas, April will be too near Easter. And when Valentine's Day comes round, is he spending it with you? No, thought not. If he has children there will also be another excuse, "Jodie's doing her GCSEs" or "My eldest is getting married and I can't go now". Here's the **Tough Love** bit - **Don't be a sucker because you're on your own and this wonderful man who happens to be in an unhappy relationship, showers you with affection.** In my view, either a man is available or he's not. It's that simple. Don't be second best, it's your life and you deserve someone who's going to put you first. Right I've said my bit, let's move on.

I was married for a long time and whilst I want to meet someone, I feel as if I want to date a lot of people first. Is that normal?

Some people get married young, have children and then just as 40 plus arrives, find they're suddenly free from a relationship for possibly the first time in 20 years. It can be scary but can be liberating. You are you, for the first time in a long time rather than being part of someone else. I've known many women who want to have fun and not go straight back into a long-term relationship. Going out with a number of people, doesn't necessarily mean sleeping with lots of them. But if that's what you want, then fine. Play the field but don't get hurt in the process. When I first divorced I came up with this strategy:

There are 52 weeks in the year, which means 52 Saturday nights. Take out the high holy days, Christmas, Summer holiday and Easter and you roughly have about 45 weekends. All of these are an opportunity to go out with someone and have dinner. After all who wants to cook and wash up on a Saturday night? I felt the whole year I did this was a numbers game. Some men I liked and even dated twice, some I couldn't even get through the first drink with. To me it was all a bit of a game, but then I wasn't ready to go back into another relationship, I just wanted to go out and have fun. I would recommend it, because not only do you meet a lot of people, you find a lot out about yourself, such as what you're looking for and what you're not. It also gives you a lot of stories to dine out on with your girlfriends.

My body isn't what it was!

Whose is? Our body changes shape, even if we've stayed the same size and weight and of course, nothing is as toned as it once was, despite regular exercise. I find a good fake tan covers a multitude of sins and makes you feel so much happier. A visit to a good lingerie shop can also work wonders, a good bra lifts, body contouring pants firm and all-in-ones smooth all over. But at the end of the day it's up to you, and whether you feel, exercise and weight change is helpful, but you're never again going to have the body of a 20 year old again.

I want to have sex, but I'm scared

The first time with your new partner should be completely mind-blowing, but this is real life so instead of the long drawn out love-making we see in films it can turn into a bit of a fumble in the dark with one, if not both of you thinking, 'Was that it?'

The first time I had sex with someone other than my husband, it lasted 10 minutes before he climaxed, and I was left wanting. Not quite the romance I dreamed of.

For all the talk of sex in the media and elsewhere, it still is filled with secrecy and to some degree embarrassment. We still find it hard to say what we want and ask what our partner may want. But telling your new partner what you like and want more of, allows you to reveal yourself, and far from being horrified, lovers tend to respond with encouragement and approval.

You may need to guide someone, and they may have to do the same for you. Some things you may find a bit odd, but ultimately you have to decide how you are going to fit together. Having sex with a new but loving partner can allow you to safely cast off your normal defenses and satisfy your longing for extreme closeness and mutual acceptance.

Nerves and not knowing what the other person wants or likes is a major reason why things start to get awkward after kissing. To relax yourself, do a lot of touching and kissing during the date, it will warm you both up for when you are alone in the bedroom. Talking about the bedroom, if you know you will probably end up there, plan in advance, put clean sheets on and clear the clutter. This allows you a clear mind to, at the appropriate time, put on the music, dim the lights and move into action. Here's a tip: get rid of photos, especially those of your children, no-one wants to see them, when trying to get in the mood.

Take it slow, foreplay and more foreplay is the name of the game; it builds excitement and relaxes you both. The slower the build-up the more the excitement. A quick warning, don't worry if you don't orgasm the first time; women nearly always set their expectations too high, must be all those romcoms. Whenever you do anything for the first time it's new and needs time to be learnt, it's the second or third time you settle into what each of you like and want.

What happens when dating goes really wrong?

It would be lovely to think the world of dating is like a big cushion - soft, fluffy and easy to sink in to. This is fantasyland. The problem with the dating game once you've been out of it for a while is it's a bloody big shock to the system. Being stood up, dumped after 20 minutes or unbearably patronized is unfortunately par for the course. You may be lucky that none of the above happens, but dating is a numbers game and there's every chance you'll stumble across it at some point.

First thing to remember is it's *Not Your Fault*. It's their loss and nothing to do with you, they're the loser here. One of the problems when you date or go out to meet someone is that you have no idea what's going on in their life. It's a bit like a job interview, you don't know who the employer's seen before, if they have someone else in mind or indeed if they really know what they're looking for. *You Don't Know* and therefore *It's Not Your Fault.*

Believe me I know the effort it takes, not only to get to the meeting place after a good hour in front of the mirror, and how tiring are the mind games we play with ourselves? 'What will we talk about?', 'Does this dress look okay?', 'Too much makeup? Too little?' But if things don't go well, put it down to experience and get back on the horse.

What happens if I'm stood up?

You're at the meeting place, probably a bar or pub, you look around, he isn't there. You wait, 5 minutes, 10 minutes, 15 minutes, now you're feeling like an idiot. First, give him a call, keep it light and breezy. It's likely you'll go straight to answerphone but even if he does pick up, play it cool. "Hi, I thought we were getting together tonight, give me a buzz back just to let me know if you are okay, speak to you soon." The reason I don't recommend you go to his house with a sharp knife and in a bad mood is because you don't want to burn your bridges, and you could end up behind bars. There can be genuine reasons why someone is late. He may have been caught in traffic and the minute you put the phone down, he walks through the door. If you've ranted on the phone, it's not going to look or sound so good when he listens to it. Playing it cool not only says to him that you aren't taking this to heart but also keeps the door open if there is a genuine reason. If he never calls you back, you know you acted like a lady and he acted like an arsehole, but that's his problem not yours.

Why is he keeping things so casual?

This could be for a number of reasons maybe he's afraid of scaring you off, he's seeing other women or a hundred other reasons that are not personally related to you. This relationship will go nowhere fast. Take the lead, tell him you want a bit more than being in the friend zone. If he wants to keep you he will make a move, if not, you make a move – in the opposite direction!

I'm scared of being rejected

Well of course you are, no-one likes to be rejected whether it's after the first date or the 20th. It's easy to drive yourself mad thinking about the big question, *why*? But dwelling on this doesn't give answers or change the fact. Sometimes in life, we don't get answers, sometimes it's better not to! It simply boils down to the fact you weren't right for them at this time in their lives and therefore it stands to reason they weren't right for you. It isn't that you weren't good enough it doesn't mean you're doomed to singledom. Take time to lick your wounds and find something else to do in the evenings with less pressure. Dating isn't a matter of international importance, have some fun with friends and heal yourself.

What if someone asks you out and you don't want to go?

I'm not sure what's worse, no-one asking you out or being asked by someone you don't want to date. It is extremely flattering to be asked but don't feel guilty for a polite "Thank you, but no." As I've said, it is hard to be rejected but it can be equally tough to be the rejecter. As women we're constantly made to feel guilty for saying no whether it's doing the washing or a date, but it isn't our duty in life to appease everyone. Being clear about saying no is better than keeping someone hanging on. If you're not clear it turns into an embarrassing situation for both you and him.You're not saying, "I don't like you", maybe you're saying like Miranda in Sex in the City, "I'm just not into you but that doesn't mean we can't be friends."

What if it's a great first date, bad second date?

The second date is really just an extension of the first date, you're still getting to know each other, you want to continue that first date experience and you haven't seen each other naked yet (right?). The second date like the first should be fun leaving room for casual conversation, but also offering the opportunity to tell stories and share thoughts, probably not on world peace, leave that till later in the relationship.

A bad second date is when you feel you're out with a totally different person from the one you saw a week ago. There are awkward pauses and you find yourself talking rubbish such as, "The toilets here are really nice." This is called second date slump. The first date is all about first impressions and there isn't a lot invested emotionally, but on the second date reality creeps in. You're getting to know someone better and the stakes are raised, intimacy becomes more real. The best way to avoid a slump is to make sure the date is low pressure, go for a pizza, bowling, even the cinema, it's low key and you won't compare it to the bells and whistles first date. The second date is one in which you can be yourself unlike the first date which is tiring because you need to be a totally dazzling version of you. But ultimately you want to date someone who likes the real you. That's not to say don't put any effort in but be authentic. Once the second date is over, whether it was another night in paradise or a complete disaster, let it go and put the focus back onto your own life. Don't sit around thinking about it, waiting for the phone to ring, get back to your own busy schedule. If he winds up being part of that – great, if not, you have a whole first date with someone else to look forward to.

I want to meet someone of my own faith

As a Matchmaker I commonly come across people who want to meet someone of their own faith. While this isn't impossible, it does decrease the pool of people you can date. Nowadays you are more likely to come across someone who was born into a faith but is now more spiritual than religious. If you are set on meeting someone of your own faith, then consider the internet dating sites or matchmakers who have faith set as a target market. Christian Connections is one, J-date (for those of Jewish faith) is another, Project 143 is a Matchmaking service for the Asian community. The good thing about dating someone from your own faith is you will already have a connection and a shared cultural background. Remember though that even those of the same faith may practice at different levels. I know people who are Jewish but don't keep kosher at home or outside and have no problem ordering a bacon sandwich. Even on the faith side you might have to compromise.

I'm not attracted to men of my own age, I want to date someone younger to reflect how I feel.

It's well know that men want to date younger women, think George Clooney and his wife Amal 17 years difference or Harrison Ford and Calista Flockhart (22 years) and even Donald Trump and Melania (23 years) and we accept the thinking that the women must be after a father figure, but what happens when you get to 50ish and you feel young so you want to go out with a guy who is young, we only have to look over the English Channel to see President Macron, 41, married to Brigitte who is 65, she certainly looks fantastically young. Whilst we accept the older male dating the younger woman the other way around is still talked about with a giggle, but hang on, the women I meet who are 40 plus normally work out, have their hair done and wear great clothes, whilst their male counterparts don't and frankly many of them have just let themselves go. There is also the believed fact that men reach their sexual prime in their late 20s whereas women in their 40s and 50s. The truth is that older women have learnt a lot about themselves and therefore can offer more to the party. Unhappily society has coined the term "cougar" and it isn't said in a pleasant positive way. If you do want to date a younger man there are benefits, he will tend to be full of energy, have less emotional worries and has been taught that housework is to be treated equally (thank you mothers). If you can date a younger guy, have something in common with him and connect sexually then go for it. All relationships have their ups and downs but there is something to be said about being the "older woman".

How do I find my mojo again?

Mojo is the quality that attracts people to you, makes you successful and full of energy. All I can say is that you will get whatever you project out and if you can build your own confidence and happiness that will shine and therefore attract people to you. If you are familiar with the Law of Attraction you will know that nothing externally can ever make us truly happy and this is really what "mojo" is. When you concentrate on yourself you can attract ideas, people and inspirations. This of course is what some people will term as selfish but this is wrong because the dictionary definition of "selfish" is having a lack of consideration for other people, having time to concentrate on yourself is not selfish, mainly because if you have kids you are lucky to get 5 minutes not to be thinking of others! But being able to find your "mojo" means that you have to think about what makes you happy and do those things so that it projects out of you. This is getting your mojo back. One of the things I recommend is that you take a piece of paper and draw three columns out. At the top of the columns put three headings; Places, People, Pain. Write underneath the places that make you happy when you go there, under people write out the names of those that make you smile, support you and you can talk to and then there is pain. Under this column you need to put what causes you pain.

Here's my example:

PLACES	PEOPLE	PAIN
London The Theatre Country pubs	My friends Julie and Leanne My sister	Argument with a friend Not getting on with my boss

The idea is that you visit the places and people that make you happy within the month and spend time there, this gives you a place of comfort and the feeling of happiness will last long after you have come away from them. With the heading of *pain* you need to set yourself of goal of doing one or even all three things, you either need to forgive, possibly need to apologies or seek professional help. We know that we attract people and situations based on our current state so we have to do something to feel as if we already have whatever it is we want. The more you feel it the easier it becomes to detach yourself from negativity and live as if you are happy and optimistic with your "mojo" being projected. If you don't take action then we just let life happen to us and you can spend your days reacting to things and not feeling in control. Getting your "mojo back" means that you start to feel better, become the best version of yourself, be in control and ready to take on new experiences

I've had a full career but somehow never found the right mate

Here's the scenario, a crowd of people are on the beach, they are all roughly the same age with similar intellect, they are chatting to others, flirting and sometimes kissing, at some point a ship pulls in, it's called HMS Marriage. The people on the beach are so excited by this ship they get on and sail off, but a few people are not on the beach, they're in the office working because they are happy at work, they are making money and beside no-one on the beach is that interesting or exciting. Consequently they "miss the boat". As a Matchmaker I meet a lot of people, some are divorced or widowed but a good many of them have had a great career but not one date in years. Now at over 40 they are standing on the beach thinking "I need to be on the next boat".

Of course, one of the main problems is that as soon as you mention your career to a guy it puts them off, instead of thinking "great, here is someone who can make decisions, be financially stable and has a great work ethic" they are actually turned off. What they really think is that you are really competitive and most probably personality Type A (common traits are competitive, achievement orientated, impatient, stressed). Most men are turned off by your success, sorry to say that, and it doesn't seem fair but there it is, they will most likely feel intimidated this is why you will find yourself at work surrounded by men but they are equally career minded, most probably married and only know you by your name and not by who you are personally. Here's the *tough love* – **if you don't slow down in your career, your social/love life won't have a chance to flourish.** I come back to the Law of Attraction, what you focus on will grow and if you keep focusing on your career it will grow and grow but it won't get you a date let alone married with children. Just a quick word though, make sure that being with someone for a relationship is something you actually want, a lot of women who have great careers want a "companion", that is not a relationship, you can't just have someone at the weekend and possibly not even then if you have a deadline to reach. If you really want a relationship you have to focus on making it happen and put your career second. That can be a hard thing to do especially as you've spent years building a reputation and respect of your colleagues. Make sure you want a relationship and are prepared to let go. Most guys don't want to be your companion or plus one, unless they are like-minded and I will tell you that the "relationship" won't be very satisfactory and definitely won't hit the buttons.

Now having decided that you do want it you are going to hate me when I say that another piece of **tough love** is – **get rid of your masculine energy.** Women who have fantastic careers are not normally girly girls, they have a masculine energy. In fact, we all have both masculine and feminine energy in us but in career focused women, who generally work in male dominated environments (banking, medical, engineering etc) they tend to not only be logical and decisive but also direct and strong. This is not attractive to men, men don't want to date a woman with masculine energy so put it away, bring out your feminine side. It may be difficult, but you are going to have to try to put time aside to find some female friends and do a few things with them to bring out your feminine side, it's not about being someone different it's about softening yourself, reduce the hard corners and enjoy life a bit more, it's in you just go and get it. Once you leave behind some of that masculine energy you will attract someone.

Here are some quick tips:

Stop winging and whining. If there's something in your life you don't like, you either have to fix it or move away from it. You can vent about it for a short while to close friends but then you have to *do* something, or it will eat you up. Do something different - take yourself out of your comfort zone. Join a group and go on your own if you can't find someone to go with.

Book a holiday or an adventure. Push yourself. It will not only give you something to talk about, but you'll feel proud of yourself. I booked to go with a Meetup group kayaking down the river Thames. Did I enjoy it? Not all of it, I was cold, my back started to hurt three strokes in but on the whole, it was a great experience, met some fab people and at least I know I can do it at the age of 53 plus. And here's the best bit not only did I feel proud of myself, but when I put it on Facebook, I was admired by all!

Wear something that really suits you, get your hair done, put your make-up on. Then go out, even if it's just a walk down the street. If you look good, you feel good.

Do something you're good at. The knowledge that you're good at something will make you tackle all the other things you need to do.

Make sure the chatterbox in your head is one that gives positive message only.

Engage in physical activity, walk, cycle, swim, play tennis. Lack of movement makes you feel lethargic, activity releases the endorphins in your brain which give you a feel-good feeling.

Even if you've failed at something, keep going. This quote has always helped me, *"You're not a failure if you don't succeed, you're a success because you've tried!"*

Be true to yourself. You can only be who you are, not what others want you to be. Look inside yourself, reflect and then move on.

Stride purposely in life, head up, shoulders back and thinking "I'm great so sod the rest of you." Works every time!

~ Good Luck! ~

A little note from me

Whether you are in your 40s, 50s or 60s it's never too late to look for and find love. Don't be put off creating a life for yourself that you truly deserve and as you are doing that the people you want to attract will walk straight in.

Commit to yourself to be the best you can and you will find that you will have the most amazing life.

Contact me anytime by emailing;

Jacqui@matchingup.co.uk

Matchmaker Jacqui on Facebook

It's always great to connect to people who have either read this book, seen my videos on YouTube (Matchmaker Jacqui) or had a coffee with me. If you would like my help in meeting someone special or some advice then contact me on the above email. I'll try my best to help you.

Can I ask you a favour? If you have enjoyed this book and you can see that it could help your life then I would like to ask you to think of someone else who might like it. Please give this book to them and ask them to read it. Or even better, buy them a copy. If you believe that you have a friend who is struggling to find a date then spread the word and share this book.

I'll leave you with a couple of quotes

"Everyone, without exception, is searching for happiness."

-Blaise Pascal

"If you don't place your foot on the rope, you'll never cross the chasm."

-Anon

References

de Botton, A., 2017. *How to find love: Essay*. 1st ed. London: The School of Life.

Buckmaster, H., 2007. *Box of Hair: A fairy tale*. 1st ed. Sacramento: Createspace.

newswire.com. 2019. */ global-facial-injectables-market-is-expected-to-worth-7-2-billion-by*. [ONLINE] Available at: http://www.newswire.com/news. [Accessed 7 November 2018].

Lewis, W. 2007. *Plastic Makes Perfect: The complete cosmetic beauty guide*. 1st ed. London: Orion

Hinsz, V. B, Matz, D. C, Patience, R.A. 2001. Does Women's Hair Signal Reproductive Potential? *Journal of Experimental Social Psychology*, 37. Vol 2, 166-172.

kent.ac.uk 2019./*top-ten-skills* [ONLINE] Available at: http://www.kent.ac.uk [Accessed 7 November 2018]

Brown, J D, Smart, S A. 1991. The Self and Social Conduct: Linking Self-Representations to Prosocial Behaviour. *Journal of Personality and Social Psychology*, 60. Vol 3, 368-375.

Jeffers, S., 1987. *Feel the Fear and do it anyway*. 1st ed. New York: Random House.

www.meetup.com

Samuel Hum. 2015. *How Tinder Obtained More Than 50 Million Users Through Word-of-Mouth*. [ONLINE] Available at: https://www.referralcandy.com/blog/tinder-marketing-strategy/. [Accessed 20 February 2019].

Elyse Romano. 2013. *The state of dating in America*. [ONLINE] Available at: https://www.datingsitesreviews.com. [Accessed 20 February 2019].

Eharmony. 2013. *The most successful online dating profile photos revealed*. [ONLINE] Available at: https://www.eharmony.com/dating-advice/using-eharmony/the-most-popular-online-dating-profile-photos-revealed/. [Accessed 21 November 2018]

Jessica Tracy. Alec Beall. 2011. *Happy guys finish last, says new study on sexual attractiveness*. [ONLINE] Available at: https://www.sciencedaily.com. [Accessed 13 November 2018].

Jeremy Nicholson. 2013. *How Can I Find a Good Man or Woman?* [ONLINE] Available at: https://www.psychologytoday.com. [Accessed 20 February 2019].

Linkedin Learning. (2018). *Seven types of people to have in your network*. 1. [ONLINE]. 13 November 2018. Available from: https://www.linkedin.com/learning/networking-for-sales-professionals/seven-types-of-people-to-have-in-your-network [Accessed: 13 November 2018].

Langlois, J H et al, 2000. Maxims or Myths of Beauty? A Meta-Analytic and Theoretical Review. *American Psychological Association Inc*, 126. Vol 3, 390 - 42

Marilyn Messik at Create Communications for images

Sarah Hutchings for image on page 8

Printed in Great Britain
by Amazon